ETERNAL AWAKENED LOVE

THAT NEVER DIES

Sarbjit Basra

Email: lovehelpserveall@hotmail.com
Instagram: @love_help_serve_all

Published July 2025 by Sarbjit Basra
Printed by Anchorprint Limited.

ISBN: 978-0-9569660-2-5

To Sandeep

Best wish

DEDICATION

"I am just a Human"
Neither a "Muslim"
Nor a "Hindu"
I am not a "Christian"
Nor a "Buddhist"
I do not belong to "Sikhism"
But my faith is "Humanity"
Therefore, my faith is "Humanity"
And "The Humanity belongs to all religions/faiths of the whole Universe"
Therefore, I love every Human of the world and love and want to serve all

Written by
Reena Pradhan

Reena Pradhan (Amma). Is a very intelligent soul who is over 80 years of age. She is very near and dear to me. Ever since we met in 2001, she has always said she wants to print a book of her writings. She has no idea yet about one of her writings has been printed in this book as a dedication to her. For her devotion and her love. Her writing speaks for it self.

Love you AMMA.

My happiness is your happiness. When you are happy so am I. When you are sad so am I. When you weep tears , so do I. For you and I are one and all that there is. Neither you nor I are separate. The only distance and difference between us is the conditioning and competitive programming. When you are ready to break down all barriers of separation, I will be waiting there with HOPE that lives in my HEART inside of me. Many times I wipe its tears each time it sees others tearing one another apart for NO MEANINGFUL REASONS. It seems as if JOY UNITY and HAPPINESS has left this EARTH. As I cannot find them ANYWHERE. Everywhere I look I see ANGER RESENTMENT and SEPARATION with EGO leading all.

If anyone is going through a rough patch at this moment of time, it will pass over. Life is full of passing CLOUDS. Everything eventually passes by teaching us something or other. Tears of Happiness or SADNESS. Everything is just a passing PHASE. When hardship CONFRONTS us, remind our self that it will teach us ACCORDINGLY to how we CHOOSE to ACT or REACT but eventually it will DISAPPEAR, leaving behind an EXPERIENCE of EMOTIONS whether it's heavy or light, happy or sad . Try not to DWELL too deep into sorrow. Life is too SHORT to drown into stress of emotions. SMILE LAUGH and be HAPPY. They are the only survivable tools. The rest will take care of itself. There is always a SILVER LINING.

When we close our eyes and learn to switch off from all outside visions and sounds, with patience we go so deep within. There you find SERENE CALMNESS. At that point we are able to inner connect with our higher self and get ANSWERS to all our QUESTIONS. Remember NO ONE knows us better than we know our selves. Otherwise we are THREE people. The one we think we are, the one others think we are, and the one we really are. We have no idea who we really are because all throughout life we have been PROGRAMMED. That is why it is very important to go within so that the INNER and OUTER CONNECTION becomes ONE. Otherwise we are strangers to our self without realising.

Someone very special loving and compassionately said to me, I need to loose my EGO. I have searched HIGH and LOW, inner and outward but I CANNOT find it ANYWHERE. I try my best to be honest and sincere. I love everyone everything and all that there is. Forgiving others and letting go of HURT and PAIN is very easy for me although I may not always forget. My love for ALL is PURE and DIVINE without EXPECTATIONS or CONDITIONS. To reach out to others in NEED brings me GREAT JOY that CANNOT be put into WORDS. To wipe others pain sorrow or tears keeps me ALIVE. I try and share with others the COMPASSION I have, just so that we can bring UNITY PEACE JOY HARMONY back into this COSMIC UNIVERSE.

Every morning is a GIFT, every moment is a present that's why we call it PRESENCE. Take a moment to realise what this means so that we can learn to RESPECT VALUE and CHERISH every moment we are given to be AMONGST our LOVED ones. Not one MOMENT should be WASTED in HATE or WASTE. Let's count our every BLESSING and live every MOMENT to the FULL. Stop focussing here and there, just FOCUS on this MOMENT. Learn to APPRECIATE and LIVE in this moment, only this moment is GUARANTEED as the next moment may never ARRIVE. Learn to find inner CONTENTMENT PEACE will follow. Open our eyes to REALITY. Life is too short PLEASE live every moment to the FULL like it's our LAST moment.

Right now we are living on two different Dimensions and frequency. The gap seems to be getting wider. No matter how much we reach out to our loved ones, if they are not willing to meet us even half way. Slowly the connections are beginning to weaken. This is why being united is so crucial at this time, but the vibrations have to be raised by living from the HEART. Stop finding faults with the ones who are putting their hand out to uplift us, because they want us in their world and life. Souls who show us pure love and affection, how can we find faults with them. Love and resentment can never flow on the same frequency or vibrations. We all have a free will to raise our vibrations by being united non judgemental and full of LOVE.

No one in life is given a GUIDE BOOK, about the survival mechanism of handling EMOTIONS and SITUATIONS to help us to handle each moment with a better easier understanding of INNER KNOWLEDGE called COMPASSIONATE LOVE that leads to WISDOM and UNDERSTANDING. So that we may be able to see and handle our lives with PATIENCE of a CALM COLLECTIVE mind without losing our temper or state of mind, but a better understanding. I have chosen to share my VIEWS of METHOD that has worked for me. I love everyone everything and ALL THAT THERE IS. Spiritual love which is PURE and DIVINE has no ATTACHMENT EXPECTATIONS or CONDITIONS. This has made my LIFE so BEAUTIFUL that has lead me to live my every moment to the FULL. Everywhere I look I see BEAUTY that lights up divine happiness pouring and radiating LOVE and LIGHT to everyone and everything that there is in this whole UNIQUE COSMIC UNIVERSE. Please feel free to email me with any questions or suggestions that may arise. Together let's shine LOVE and LIGHT that will IGNITE UNITY amongst us. Let's be KIND to one ANOTHER so that our HEARTS will expand COMPASSION

Some souls may be wondering why I keep putting up these spiritual messages. It's because I care about the cosmic universe and I also care very deeply about you. We have no choice but to bring in GOOD CHANGES especially UNITY. Look all around us, the whole world is in CHAOS and if we refuse to make even small compassionate changes then there may not be anything left for our FUTURE GENERATIONS. We have ALL got a ROLE to play at such a time of DESPERATE NEED to HOLD HANDS and become UNITED. Deep down under the layers, WE ARE ALL GOOD KIND UNDERSTANDING INTELLIGENT SOULS who are having a HUMAN EXPERIENCE. We are all intelligent enough to know what is RIGHT and WRONG.

If I could bring one change it would be a plead to the ones who are willing to compromise to throw away EGO and ARROGANCE. We do not need such thoughts or habits that keep us separated from one another. Seriously there is NOTHING else in life more powerful than UNITY. Other wise life is what?, when we judge, point fingers trying to prove a point, although we may be totally in the wrong gear of low vibrational thoughts. What have we got to lose if we can learn to meet one another half way. What is our gain by trying to PROVE a point, if it's going to separate us by putting distance between one another. My PLEAD is LIFE is too SHORT, we may not be here for long. PLEASE DO NOT BECOME A SLAVE TO EGO.

We should try our up most best to stay level headed. When we have our highs in life, keep our feet firmly grounded. When we face our lows then we need to raise our energy and vibrations high. Be polite and pleasant to others around us. If someone smiles then given them a bigger smile back with gratitude. If someone chooses to ignore us, still give them a smile and a silent whisper of best wishes and wish them well. At this moment of time there is a lot of confusion as no one really knows what's going on, so everyone is trying their best to do what's called survival. Let's be there for one another. Help support to uplift others around us. It costs nothing to lend a helping hand.

Think twice before hurting or letting anyone down. Never play with another's feelings. Intentionally or unintentionally. More importantly DO NOT use anyone for our own benefits and then FORGET everything they did for us. One time can be an ERROR but to do it repeatedly is very wrong. Don't feel making others look small is a winning game. You win some but you loose some. What we sow is what we reap. Always try to be humble and considerate showing Gratitude each time someone holds out their helping hand, remember they didn't have to help us, just like the many who didn't offer. NEVER EVER USE ANYONE. Life should be loving appreciating supporting and respecting ONE ANOTHER.

Sometimes one has to lose its self to find one's self. That is called inner growth. There are also times we lose our selves trying so hard to fit in or trying to please others. This is not a healthy path for anyone to reach a state where you may lose your self completely. When we feel we need to change for others, then they are not the right or healthy relationships. Yes we should try our best to be honest true kind and sincere and the right souls will appreciate us as we are and would not swap us for the world. The whole cosmic universe is full of special souls to suit each and everyone. Always shine out our inner personality and be very proud of who we are. Being alive it self is a magical blessing.

There may come moments in life where one by one our loved ones start to distance them selves from us, some we may not see or hear from. When others choose to walk out of our lives then we need to respect them because we all have a free will to do what feels right for each individual. As much as it may hurt or may be HEARTBREAKING we still have to respect them by sending them lots of LOVE and LIGHT with WELL WISHES. However, we can still LOVE them from AFAR. Real pure spiritual love does not DIMINISH . That is why DETACHED LOVE is very POWERFUL. No expectations no conditions no strings. If we can learn to have no EXPECTATIONS then we will never get DISAPPOINTED.

Have we ever taken a crucial moment to go deep within to find out , what would really make us HAPPY where we may feel complete. Something that is for our HIGHEST GOOD, that lasts and does not FIZZLE AWAY. It has to be something that is a WOW effect that changes us, our surroundings and the way we act and behave, but most importantly, others around us benefit too. It should have no beginning or an ending. With no highs or lows but well balanced frequency that remains the same throughout. Then ask ourself will it make an ENORMOUS change and a GAIN. Will that gain uplift us or DRAIN us. Will we loose more than we gain to ACHIEVE. Our mind tricks us into locations where we lose our WAY and DIRECTIONS

The moment we stop judging others by expanding our mind, which then becomes OPEN MINDSET. We start to look around and there is no one or anything that we resent or feel separated from. Pure Divine LOVE starts to pour inside all our senses like sweet nectar. We start seeing the whole cosmic universe from our third eye (PINEAL GLAND). Everywhere we look we see nothing but COMPASSION BEAUTY and LOVE. Appreciating everyone everything and ALL THAT THERE IS. That is the moment where we start living to the FULL. We want to shout to the whole cosmic universe and everyone HOW MUCH WE LOVE them. Our love at that point becomes PURE and DIVINE. Try it just once to taste the NECTOR.

Could it be possible that some souls for various reasons choose to keep well away from the AWAKENED SOULS. Who have gone through so much of transformation that radiate purity and wisdom. Their AURA lights up the darkness, taking away negativity in silence. All these souls are yearning for, is to bring unity amongst one another. Setting an example of being happy and content despite living in the same atmosphere as the ones who choose to be blinded hiding their vision. There is so much to be grateful for but some choose to ERASE unity peace joy happiness harmony contentment bliss and the list goes on. WAKE up and realise that LIFE is TOO SHORT. Let all HEARTS sing out HAPPINESS.

Start each day with Gratitude and sincereness, that who ever or what ever crosses our path we welcome and see them without EGO or JUDGEMENT but with deep inner connection of warmth LOVE which is the real WORSHIP towards ALL THAT THERE IS. That what we feel and how we feel comes from the SOUL and not just the HEART as at times the heart can be lead by the mind feelings and emotions. Only the soul stands SOLID, as it is PURE and DIVINE. Once we have discovered that we are not the MIND the BODY or SENSES then comes forward only the SOUL. The soul is ETERNAL. It is full of DIVINE LOVE and LIGHT, that leads us through any DARKNESS that may try to OVER SHADOW us through life. SO KEEP SHINING so BRIGHT.

When we hurt others, knowing or unknowingly. Do we have a CONSCIENCE. If we do, then we will feel GUILTY that it will start to eat us up inside, making us feel restless. We have no right to mess with other's EMOTIONS or FEELINGS. Instead we should try to be kind considerate and understanding . Learn to be patient and wise. There is TALKING to OTHERS and TALKING AT EACH-OTHER. Our real personality shows through our ACTIONS. We may have grown up in age but have we grown up in our CHARACTER towards others. There is listening but not hearing. Let's try our best to make small GOOD changes towards one another. It costs NOTHING to be POLITE PLEASANT KIND and CONSIDERATE.

Gratitude is appreciating people and things, anything and everything that we have been blessed. Always remember BLESSED with, because we came into this world with nothing. Everything we have is given to us to use whilst on this earth. We feel we OWN this and that, in reality WE DO NOT OWN ANYTHING. NO matter what we wish to believe, otherwise why do we leave everything behind, including our BODY. The only thing that leaves is our (SOUL). Energy frequency vibrations. The one thing we may be able to say we own is our RESPECT of how we act and behave towards others. Respect is given by others, but we have to EARN it, by how we TREAT OTHERS. Be kind to OTHERS.

Have we thought or wondered who we rally are. Everything of who and what we are is all inside of us. Our organs soul emotions feelings, it's all inside. The only outer world connection we have are the tiny dots in our eye pupils, so tiny and small yet through them we have become a vision and apart of this BIG WIDE world. Yet our SOUL breath organs are all inside of our body. How is this possible, it's like peeping through a key hole. We need to question this. We are so engrossed with a world where we can smell hear see and eat connections off the outer world yet we are inside of our body. Everything that is released outer is all a waste even our TEARS. So once again WHO are we, WHAT are we. Everything inside is REALITY.

If we listen very carefully, we can hear other's pain. Blowing softly through their broken heart, no one willing to give their time or attention. Too many souls listen only from their ears but soon as we start listening with the HEART, we can hear every word like a sad musical note coming from their soul. Crying out HELP, I'm dying from what's happening all around us. Everyone going on with their own emotions and thoughts.

Without giving a thought to another. What has happened to this BIG wide world. It is so big yet very empty and lonely. Others walk each other by as if all are invisible.

From being Beautiful loving caring understanding warm souls, we are turning into separated judgemental cold souls, forgetting WHO WE are.

When are we going to start making changes by listening to one another by lending a helping hand. To care and share. Take and make time because we actually do care. Life is not only about us, or that it owes us anything. We need to take off our ARROGANCE and EGOS. Start being who we have been sent here to be. Is to be kind and considerate. Stop bickering twisting and arguing, seeing wrong where it does not belong or exist. We are not setting a GOOD example for COMPASSION to flourish, what is needed right now is UNITY amongst ALL and everyone. The ones who may not agree, need to question, as to WHY NOT. TIME is running out so QUICKLY. We may not GET ANOTHER CHANCE EVER AGAIN.

One day we may look back and regret from not taking up this very PRECIOUS SHORT TIME we are born here to bring peace joy harmony so that together we can form a UNITY. We are all ONE. We have nothing that we own except love and respect we can give to one another. More importantly is TIME. Bring joy fun and laughter for our children to see, experience and to carry it on to their children. One day when we may not be here any more because our time here may have ran out. At least let's leave a LEGACY of PEACE JOY HARMONY FUN and LAUGHTER knowing we left this earth as a BEAUTIFUL SAFE HAVEN playground for others who lived their LIVES to the FULL, because we made changes for them to follow by our EXAMPLES.

No words can express how much I love this whole cosmic universe and all that there is. I care about each one of you, why, because we are all connected together as one. We are all here on borrowed time. Nothing belongs to us here on this earth, we live moment to moment, day to day collecting things and possessions, like we are going to remain on this earth for eternity. Everything here on this earth DOES NOT BELONG TO ANY OF US. However we are able to make use of anything and everything whilst we are here on this earth. All we are doing is passing things onto generations. Convincing our selves and our loved ones, programming them to believe that the things we are handing over to them, that the OWNERSHIP belongs to us. This is our OVERCONFIDENCE of EGO. We are all well aware that we came with nothing and will leave with nothing. We are also very AWARE that we are here for a LIMITED period of time and that just like others we will leave this earth plane. Like the previous souls who came and went. It is the MINE and THINE along with our EGOS that has caused the SEPARATION between MANKIND, that led to GREED. Never having enough that all our life is spent on ACCUMULATING material gains THAT WE DO NOT OWN. Soon as we realise this reality. Our whole concept changes towards one another. There is enough in this world for everyone. We do not need to steal or tear one another apart to use what has been provided by Mother Earth, for us to use whilst we walk on this land. This cosmic universe is no more than a play ground set up as a STAGE, where we are all playing a ROLE. No one is following the SCRIPT. Which is to be kind and pleasant. Caring and sharing. Considerate understanding wise and compassionate, but what are we doing is busy judging criticising pointing fingers where ever we can, without a thought of compassion. It seems as if this has become a trend on this earth. Souls loose their tempers very easily. Listening to others is a thing of the past. They can't seem to wait for an explanation before they are ready like a lion to pounce on the innocent souls, as they seem to be easy target. Righteousness seems to have left this earth. If we do not bring unity in soon then this whole wide beautiful world will be destroyed by our resentment arrogance ego of ACTIONS. However it is not too late to nip it in the bud. I am certain and confident that there are many souls who are desperate and are yearning to form unity. To bring in peace and harmony so that we can make this a safe haven for our children and so forth. We all have a DUTY OF CARE TOWARDS ONE ANOTHER. So what are we waiting for. Let us ALL BEGIN. No time like the PRESENT which is a GIFT.

Everyone is on their own life journey, unknown moments occur where we don't always have the answers. There is no guide book. At times things may not go according. Some moments will make us, some will break us. We never stop learning. There can be rough and tough times where we won't be able to turn back the hands of time. Or say "if only I could get another chance". GUESS WHAT.. Yes we have another chance and the moment is NOW. Live life to the full like it's our last moment. Scream or yell, "I'M GOING TO LIVE EACH MOMENT TO THE FULL". Do what makes you HAPPY!. Never put off tomorrow for something that can be done today. We all have a right to be HAPPY. But not at the EXPENSE of another's HAPPINESS.

We stress about this and that. We arrived here on this cosmic earth
(playground). To run around as free spirits to have FUN. Make friends
to hear and tell MAGICAL stories that can touch so many HEARTS and
LIVES. We should be happy smiling flowing around like whispering wind,
in peace and harmony with our selves and others. Our hearts wavering
loving Melodies for all nature to become a part of. Radiating blissful love
and light shinning everywhere. To live in this world being FREE SPIRITS.
Being free means no attachments but having full access to all that there
is. As all belongs to the cosmic universe. We changed the script. We have
turned everything into a BOXING RING, where violence and crimes RULE.

How I wish I could whisper in others ears. The softness of angelic language we have all become DEAF to. The language of the HEART which is PURE LOVE. So selfless and eternal, so POWERFUL and yet so WEAK to some. We all have a free will, to what goes through our VISION of all that there is. How I wish I could make another see what I see. A heaven full of Angels playing a united melody that lingers everywhere together as ONENESS. No one SEPARATE from another. A golden smile that dazzles through the hearts of millions who radiate bliss love and light. Wiping out all the darkness that there is. These special beings called angels are you and I. We just need to put our angelic armours back on and radiate LOTS of LOVE.

Life is so BEAUTIFUL, we can close our eyes and go into deep BLISSFUL TRANCE . Where we loose all outside noise. Everything goes silent as we start hearing silence, taking us even deeper into tranquillity. Where we slip into another world. Everything pauses. It's called DYING while we are LIVING. It makes one come MORE ALIVE. Where we start APPRECIATING everyone and everything. Cherishing EACH MOMENT, each breath that we are blessed to take. We have become so DEMANDING that GRATITUDE has become WORTHLESS. Each passing day we are going further away from being WHO we really are. We are a SPIRITUAL being having a HUMAN EXPERIENCE. Forgetting our MANNERS.

Each day I am trying to understand with deep thoughts as to why souls drift away from one another. One moment they are the closest one can become, then further along they start avoiding each other, seeing the opposite of what was once upon a time. How can we make others understand the importance of life. Which is happiness and laughter. How can we not be happy. How can we not love and respect one another. Being bitter and resentful is not the nature of mankind. The universe created man to be kind considerate compassionate and understanding. So what happened along the way of wisdom, where somehow EGO slipped in and ARROGANCE took the lead. WHY CAN THIS NOT BE REVERSED.

How many have experienced both tears of joy and tears of heartache and pain?

The tears of pain cut like a knife; the pain is so unbearable. It's impossible to explain the symptoms you feel inside. Your whole world has collapsed and fallen apart.

However, the tears of gratitude and joy -

You close your eyes, and suddenly the outside world's noise and sound fade away. All you feel is relaxed, blissful; your heartbeat slows down, taking in slow, long, comfortable, in-depth breaths.

An angelic voice inside very softly whispers, "Hey, this is paradise. This is heaven."

You just want to stay in that transformational state of consciousness.

Believe me, you don't want to open your eyes knowing you are about to step back into a world full of dramatic actions.

What is LOVE, love is not linked with the mind body or senses, where there are strings conditions and expectations attached. Worldly love is attached to feelings and emotions, with a high and low sense of feelings. When we get our own way it shoots up high and when the opposite it drops low. Spiritual love is pure and divine, comes from the soul (ATMA). It has no conditions. It has a cosmic flow where you just want to radiate love and light, where ever you look and go. No strings no expectations but that feeling of wanting to radiate that magical substance, that cannot be seen. It brings out the best of our highest self beyond any means. Try loving others selflessly and unconditionally with no strings or expectations. Especially without a return.

Do we spend more time thinking about our departed ones, that we may forget to focus on the ones who care and love us dearly, that are living and walking amongst us. When did we last take a moment to see and realise, but mostly appreciate the ones who take time out for us, who may have our best interest at heart. We don't always see things as they are, because of the frame of our own minds. The ones who are sweet on the outside, we notice more. Than the ones who may be more sweet inside. Who we can count on at any time. Should we not take time to see reality of our own actions, where we may forget to tell the souls that we love,care and appreciate their presence in our lives, and that they make our lives Beautiful and worth living.

Our path is made up of little thought pebbles. Each thought we bring into our mind creates the path. Negative thoughts may create only stones and rocks. However fun laughter kindness gratitude and unity, will blossom our path . The more happy we are, the more paradise we are creating for ourself, our future and for our loved ones. Once they have walked on our creation of divine magical path, they too will wish to create something similar. Why have we complicated our path, when it's very simple to bring in the soothing magic, where everyone benefits. Let's all take small loving compassionate steps on our selves, creating our path with positive considerate thoughts and actions towards others.

Real happiness is within formed by our feelings and actions, created by how our thoughts see our every incident as it takes place. It's very important to be the master of our minds and not a slave to our desires. Every action that takes place will always be half full or half empty. We all have a choice of free will. Sometimes the action is not to hurt or belittle us, however we will choose to receive it on the action of the state of our own mind and thoughts, at the precise moment. Remember, it's not the mouth it's come out from, but the mind it's gone into. There are lots of compassionate souls who have our best interest at heart. However, there are those of different vibrations. Please do not react. It's better to keep it small than to give our power away. Be the master.

We learn so much from one another, there is always room for expansion, there is NO ONE who knows everything. When we meet other souls, there may be something that we may take away from them, that may one day become our biggest survival shield. When others take their time to interact with us. Listen very carefully, and learn to HEAR what valuable asset, they may be sharing for our own highest good. Most souls listen, but don't hear. We learn so much from one another, should we choose to listen. Learn to respect and value when we are in the company of others, who have chosen and taken time to be in our company. Everything in life should have an impact of GRATITUDE and RESPECT (it's called UNITY).

Are we certain that the things and situations, we may be searching for, will actually fulfil our contentments. Or we may not even need them, but our yearning has over taken the real reality. We don't realise how programmed we are, searching for things we don't have, that we forget to appreciate what we are already Blessed with. Our whole life may flash by, but our desires have no ending. It's the wants and desires, that start having an impact on our health peace joy happiness and relationships. Question, to gain one thing, how much we are losing. Every time a desire arises, ask (do I need it). If it's worth losing sleep health happiness and maybe relationships, then it's got to be something so unique, but non existent. Don't waste time as time is an essence.

Why is it VERY IMPORTANT to try to bring UNITY back amongst us all. Yes our lives are very fast and can be stressful, all the more reasons to be united. Problem halved can be a problem solved. So many souls are leaving this earth plane. That can be one of us, nothing is guaranteed. We will take nothing with us, so why not make small changes by reaching out to others. If nothing SMILE at someone. Ask how are you, Is that too much to make someone's day. We are called MANKIND, so where has all the kindness disappeared to. Please let's take small steps towards one another. Compassionately and selflessly. What are we going to lose. These ACTIONS will actually UPLIFT us and our souls. Just a simple smile if nothing else.

Why peace, joy, and harmony are very important to me—more so, unity is at the top. Because no one has taught us the real importance of who we really are and what life is about.

It was never meant to be a competitive race to see who can achieve more—name, fame, wealth, status. It's about our health and peace of mind.

When was the last time we actually sat down for a mental rest? Looked around to see what we may have already achieved: compassionate relationships—parents, children, friends, etc.

Relationships are the most important asset one can achieve, by appreciating, respecting, and making time for one another. Fond memories are what we will take with us, while everything else will remain behind.

If we wish to be happy and content then we need to make changes in the way we ACT, BEHAVE and CONDUCT ourself.

Never separate ourself from another, that comes through NOT JUDGING others.

Become DETACHED (not allowing anyone or anything having a hold over us), control our GREED, wanting more than what we may need. Learn to forgive others so that we can release ourselves by turning RESENTMENT and HATRED into compassion and love. All these changes make our travel in life light and easy (less Baggage easy travel).

Most times we accumulate unnecessary STRESS, it shortens our LIFESPAN. Loving and respecting others makes us better souls and makes us feel GOOD. Learn to understand others BETTER.

The moment we learn to appreciate and love others, we no longer resonate with lower vibration thoughts (Negative). We begin to see GOOD in everyone around us, as there is good in everyone. At that point when our own VIBRATIONS begin to raise, we must learn to protect our frequency. We start feeling either tired or uplifted in the company of others. That is when we decide, how much time we choose to share our company with other souls. When we are uplifted, we feel completely different, positive and happy. We start laughing more. Our awareness sharpens so that we notice our surroundings. ENERGY is souls most valuable asset that operates us. Be WISE who we choose to share our energy with.

Ways to identify WALKING ANGELS among us, that we see in every day life. Soon as they walk into a room they uplift the frequency and vibrations, very selfless and forgiving.

They touch others HEARTS and LIVES, you will notice a beautiful glow on their face with a calming far away look that they live here on earth and on other dimensions at the same time.

They do not have wings that can be seen with human eyes, but they walk and live amongst us all the time. They have the ability to change our fate, destiny and make the impossible possible. They are full of love passion and compassion, never getting tired or worn out, full of energy that lights up magic where ever they go.

Never use or abuse these special souls in DISGUISE.

Try our best to stay positive by uplifting the vibrations from focusing on good Positive things and events that take place in our lives.

The not so good events allow things to fall out from our mind and thoughts so it allows space and room for happiness, fun, laughter joy , and sensational feelings and emotions that will uplift us and have a POSITIVE impact on our HEALTH and PEACE of MIND.

Never dwell on others moods or ACTIONS. Their actions have nothing to do with us, it's who they are and how they may be going through their own personal path of experiences.

Care about others and be there at times of need but DO NOT carry their EMOTIONS by giving our POWER to their attitude and BEHAVIOUR towards us, instead send out our LOVE and LIGHT.

Every morning is a GIFT, every moment is a present that's why we call it PRESENCE. Take a moment to realise what this means so that we can learn to RESPECT, VALUE and CHERISH every moment we are given to be AMONGST our LOVED ones.

Not one MOMENT should be WASTED in HATE or WASTE, let's count our every BLESSING and live every MOMENT to the FULL. Stop focusing here and there, just FOCUS on this MOMENT. Learn to APPRECIATE and LIVE in this moment, only this moment is GUARANTEED as the next moment may never ARRIVE.

Learn to find inner CONTENTMENT and PEACE will follow. Open our eyes to REALITY, life is too short so PLEASE live every moment like it's our LAST moment.

What saddens me, is what's happening all around us, how it's so easy to judge others without having the full facts , besides we have no right to judge anyone.

When we learn the real meaning of LOVE, we would never wish to hurt anyone, life is about supporting and uplifting one another and about caring and sharing, not just our family and friends but anyone who needs a helping hand if we are in a position to help them.

Small gestures is all it takes, surely there is more to life than just filling our own pockets, where are we going to take our full pockets to? Because we won't be able to take anything with us when it's time TO LEAVE, why can we not turn RESENTMENT into UNITY?

WHY HURT ANYONE? HOW CAN WE SEE ANYONE IN PAIN?

The reason I write these spiritual affirmations and have decided to print them as a book is because I live and love my life to the full and my aim is to encourage other like minded souls to see what works for me as none of us are born with a GUIDE BOOK.

I CARE and LOVE everyone and everything and all that there is in this whole COSMIC UNIVERSE, why? Because I know that I am ONENESS with everything and all that there is.

I live my life to the FULL as every MOMENT for me is a BLESSING (GIFT), hoping it encourages others to start living their lives to the full so that together we can bring UNITY, LOVE and LIGHT back into our LIVES and into this WHOLE COSMIC UNIVERSE.

Never gain anything at another's LOSS, never hurt anyone intentionally, never cheat to gain, only lie if it's a matter of life or death.

Try to be honest and sincere as that is our real identity, when we cheat another, we are cheating our self, help others in need selflessly and unconditionally. Put a SMILE on another's face, buy someone food, give someone way when driving, become someone's strength and wipe someone's TEARS.

Call someone who may be lonely, take someone shopping who has no car, stop judging others, don't use or abuse one another.

Don't take anything that does not belong to us, if we can't make someone laugh then don't make them cry neither, try not to hurt anyone but uplift them instead.

If I'm to view Mother Earth, she is very selfless. Her love is unconditional, wanting nothing in return for allowing us to live here.
She has provided us with more than we could expect or have needed. We poke her, disturb and hurt her; we do all sorts of unkind things, knowingly or unknowingly.

When was the last time we offered our gratitude?
Mother Earth is like a big playground where she wants to see all her children happy, playing around without a care in the world—having free, fun minds and quality time being united with one another.

She wants us all to smile at others and occasionally give others a spiritual hug. Hugging someone compassionately is medicine. It takes away pain and tears. Erases heartache and pain.

Life is as beautiful as the thoughts that we allow to enter our minds. Positive, loving, compassionate thoughts come along with a shining rainbow with a silver lining. Low vibration thoughts will have the opposite effect. We are in the driving seat, responsible to master our mind and thoughts.

There is so much to be grateful for.
Take a good look around us - everywhere lies beauty: beauty within and beauty outside.

Let's remove the low vibration thoughts and ideas so that the magic begins to manifest into reality. Real happiness and contentment are inside each and every one of us.

Then why are we searching for them high and low outside? Let's learn to appreciate all that there is.

Real happiness is within, formed by our feelings and actions, created by how our thoughts perceive every incident as it takes place. It's very important to be the master of our minds and not a slave to our desires. Every action that takes place will always be seen as half full or half empty. We all have a choice of free will.

Sometimes the action is not meant to hurt or belittle us; however, we choose to receive it based on the state of our own mind and thoughts at that precise moment. Remember, it's not the mouth it comes from, it's the mind it goes into.

There are lots of compassionate souls who have our best interests at heart. However, there are those of different vibrations. Please do not react; it's better to keep it small than to give our power away. Be the master.

Some may see me as crazy or mad, but I see myself as a spiritual soul who has lived endless lifetimes to come into this human form to RADIATE SPIRITUAL LOVE and LIGHT, at a time when this WHOLE COSMIC UNIVERSE is CRUMBLING, all due to our own ATTITUDE and ACTIONS towards everything and everyone.

We are so quick to judge and point fingers without taking a moment of compassionate understanding.

Who are we? What are we? Why are we really here? Why did we come with nothing and will leave with nothing? All these relationships will either go before us or be left behind, along with all this wealth we keep hoarding.

That's what we mainly focus on.
Ask again: Who are we and why are we here?

When others take their time to interact with us, listen very carefully and learn to HEAR what valuable asset they may be sharing for our own highest good.

Most souls listen but don't hear. We learn so much from one another should we choose to listen. Learn to respect and value when we are in the company of others who have chosen and taken time to be with us.

Everything in life should have an impact of GRATITUDE and RESPECT.

What if I was to tell you that real happiness and contentment is inside of each and everyone of us, and you asked me to give you proof.

First can we see the air that we breathe. Can we see the electric each time we switch on anything electrical etc. I would then say this is how we have been programmed (seeing is believing).

There are things that cannot be seen but have to be felt. Close our eyes slow our breathing and bring our mind to listen to our breathing. Slowly you will start to feel so calm and collective.

That is the beginning of peace then harmony will follow. Slowly with practice we begin to identify who and what we really are. Yet in this very crazy fast world we have lost our selves. Worn out and tired chased by stress. With no ending to desires.

Life is like building castles in the sand. We are rushing around trying to accomplish and accumulate as many material gains as we can.

Yes, we need all these things, but never allow them to overtake our mind's health, especially peace.

Slow down and start to enjoy other things too. Happiness, peace, joy, and harmony are the most important ingredients needed for us to function properly in our everyday life.

Our health is our wealth. Don't burn your candle at both ends. We cannot put a price on our health or time.

Let's spend our time on this earth being wise toward everything, everyone, and most importantly, toward our own selves.

Life is so very short—please don't forget to enjoy every moment.

Nothing else is guaranteed.

I am not here to judge or to point fingers at anyone. Life is too short to waste even a moment. We are all so blessed to be here on this Mother Earth, and I for one wish to spend every moment in Gratitude. Appreciating everything and everyone, who I have been so blessed to have in my life. I never wish to abuse or use anything or anyone. I am here for anyone who may need a helping hand or a listening ear. Please feel free to contact me at time of need. We may never get on with everyone, so if that is the case I wish everyone good wishes and send lots of spiritual love and light. Everyone deserves to be happy as life is too short. Don't waste a moment. Be happy always. My Blessing to everyone .

If my mind were to ask my conscience what makes me happy, my sincere reply would be to see unity amongst all my brothers and sisters, as the whole cosmic universe is all one. To care and share, to uplift one another by making others laugh. Have fun, make good happy jokes. To let everyone know how important each and every one is. How my life would be empty without them. How they make my life complete and worth living.

Every crack of dawn is beyond reach if it wasn't for the spiritual love that surrounds us all, which we have been blinded to see. Yet I see that spiritual love I have for this whole cosmic universe. We are all supreme divine love and light—not the mind, the body, or the senses. We are a soul (ATMA), full of spiritual love.

Have we ever taken a moment to study and understand reality? Who are we? Why are we here? How and why did we come into this world naked, with nothing - not even clothes? And then one day, as guaranteed, we will leave behind even our body, while our soul will return as it came.

The question is: we have been programmed to compete, fight, argue, and judge one another. Some souls don't even know what it's like to be happy, content, or to smile at another. Gratitude does not even come into the equation.

We often fail to recognise who our loved ones are - those who try their best to help and support us in times of need. Right now, there is so much separation. Yet, it only takes one person to want to make compassionate, positive changes - for unity to arise.

Together, we can bring unity back.

We woke up this morning, did we thank the universe for yet another Glorious Beautiful day, or did we only focus on negative thoughts, that are not positive for our highest good. Our thoughts create the path we choose to walk on, so choose your thoughts very wisely, where we and others around us benefit in our health and mental state of mind. Our mind is the most powerful tool that, it can MAKE US OR BREAK US. Don't rush. Always try and keep a clear positive and compassionate mind.

Our mind is the most powerful tool; it can make us or break us.

Don't rush. Always try to keep a clear, positive, and compassionate mind.

Life can be difficult at times—sometimes filled with heartache, pain, and stress. It's during those times that we need a compassionate voice to give us strength, not to judge or tear us apart.

It costs nothing to help uplift another. Do it through compassion and love, with no strings, expectations, or conditions. Do it selflessly because we care and are compassionate enough to lend a helping hand.

How long does it take to call someone for a quick "hi" and then "bye"?

We never know who may be suffering alone in silence, as many souls find it very difficult to open up because of the times we are all living in at this very moment.

We have to make a difference by bringing changes in the way we act and behave towards other souls.

Please make small, compassionate, spiritual changes.

Real love is pure and divine; it comes from the soul to the soul. It has no beginning or end. That kind of love is eternal and everlasting.
It is the most powerful source of existence in this reality we are blessed to be a part of.

The most amazing and magical moment is when we can wipe away another's tear, share their burden or pain, and give them hope by smiling and saying, "It's going to be okay," and that they are not alone. To share our torch of light in times of their darkness.

To help clothe someone, or to share our food with another who may not be as fortunate as ourselves in a moment of their life - this is what gives our own lives meaning. To live for another makes our life worth living; that moment brings us alive.

Help those in need at the right times, but do not allow yourself to be used - helping is not about being a doormat. We are a cushion for genuine moments of need, for those who may be in difficult situations through no fault of their own.

Caring and sharing is the most selfless and unconditional act, an experience that words can never truly capture.

Never stop being who you are, no matter how much negative energy tries to suffocate the love and compassion you wish to share with the rest of the world.

It takes a bigger person to reach out and uplift another—even a simple smile can become someone's medicine. So many souls are suffering in silence, feeling that something is missing, some not even understanding the emptiness they feel. Suffering comes in many different forms and ways.

Share your torch of unity with them. Send a good thought filled with spiritual love and light. When we care and share selfless thoughts and wishes for others in need, it brings a joy that cannot be put into words.

Try it - just once.

Lots of souls may get fed up with my posts. However, I'm not going to give up trying to bring peace, joy, harmony, and unity among us - so that we can make this a better place for our children and generations to come.

It only takes one person to make small changes - in the way we see life, the way we act, behave, and conduct ourselves in response to what we witness with our eyes and conscience. Is it really that hard to stop judging? There is good in everyone; it all depends on what we choose to notice and see.

Life is too short to live in misery, moaning and groaning. If we don't make small positive changes, our lives will pass us by like a fast-forward switch.

Don't we all deserve to smile, laugh, and have fun each and every day?

What a beautiful world we have been blessed with - along with special relationships, whether they are blood-related or otherwise. We should ask ourselves how much importance we truly give to them. We often take each moment, along with most things, for granted.

Once we learn to value and appreciate, everything around us suddenly becomes alive - and in that process, we start coming alive too. Our senses begin to play their role, allowing us to truly identify our feelings and emotions. That is called life.

How many souls can honestly say they are happy and living their life to the fullest in the present moment? The present moment is all that is guaranteed - and that's why it's so important to be mindful of how we choose to live it. Whether it's the company we keep or the surroundings we're in - choose very wisely.

Don't waste a moment.

We are all blessed with so many things we have been Blessed with. We count money calories steps etc. Then why do we not count our Blessings.

There are many souls who would love to be in our shoes. There are so many, that are less fortunate than us, who carry on with life smiling counting their blessings. Less BAGGAGE easy TRAVEL. Next time we overlook to appreciate. Take a moment to look around your surroundings. Take a deep breath and be sincere to send out Gratitude. Even for little things and events in our lives.

We can barely cope with what we have been blessed with, yet we are yearning for more. The reason we may not have what we yearn for, is because we did not need it. Remember less baggage easy travel.

If you're reading this, you are one of the special souls who can help bring positive change to this cosmic universe. Together, we can create peace, joy, harmony, and unity.

There should be no crime or violence—that is not the reason we have been blessed to walk on this beautiful Mother Earth. She is full of love and is yearning for us to change our mindset: the way we think, act, and behave toward one another.

Is that too much to ask in return for being allowed to walk on this Earth we call home?

Right now, there is so much separation among humankind. Even the stars above seem to ask, "Why is man so unhappy and unkind to one another?" That's when their tears begin to fall as rain.

We woke up today, what a blessing to see yet another day. Think about the millions who did not make it to see today. Please do not waste even a moment of this precious moment as the next moment is not guaranteed, what we make of our life is up to each and everyone of us, as real happiness and contentment is within each and everyone of us. Formed by each one's thinking concept.

Remember the glass is either half full or half empty. You have a choice. We all have a choice to master our monkey mind. Don't deprive this moment stressing about tomorrow, as we may not be here. So why waste this precious moment which is a GIFT. Live your life to the full like it's your last moment.

When we leave this Earth plane, what do we take with us? The body, fully clothed, is either burnt or buried in the ground. So once again, what do we take with us? Then what are we fighting and arguing about? Why not use this time to be happy and content, as real happiness is within each and every one of us. Our health is our wealth.

The one who is awakened realizes that WE ARE ALL ONE. Nothing is more important than being there for one another, as seeing others happy is our happiness. On our own, we are nothing, but together we are EVERYTHING. We are nothing, yet everything. What does that say?

Stop wasting time drowning in negative thoughts, as they will turn into POISON. We may end up drinking that poison if changes are not made.

If I could wish for one wish, it is to bring unity among all. To change resentment and hate into unity, love, and compassion. There is no greater importance in this whole cosmic universe than unity - to uplift one another. Have a laugh and joke, eat together, care and share. Be happy for one another. Stop competing, as this is tiring and creates separation we have been programmed to live by.

Let's make good changes before it's too late. Life is too short for separation. Please wake up and see reality: WE DO NOT OWN ANYTHING. Stop judging and come together to make this world a beautiful place for ourselves, our children, and their children. Let's live by EXAMPLE. Don't be too proud to tell someone you love them and miss them.

Never stop or change from being who you are, no matter how much negative energy tries to suffocate the love and compassion you wish to share with the rest of the world.

It takes a bigger person to put their hand out to help uplift another. Even a simple smile can become someone's medicine. So many souls are suffering in silence, feeling something missing - some not even knowing the emptiness - suffering in so many different forms and ways.

Share your torch of unity with them. Send them a good thought of spiritual love and light. When we care and share selfless thoughts and wishes toward others in need, it brings back great joy that cannot be put into words. Try it, just once…

Why is it important to help one another at this moment of time, if we are in a position to, reaching out to someone and those in need is a very humble gesture.

Helping is not allowing others to use us or take advantage of our good nature.

So many souls are suffering in silence, some from health , relationships, financial need or mental health. Some do not have the courage to bring themselves to ask.

We should be aware on the look out where we may be able to uplift someone, wipe their tears, share their pain, so many different ways where we can lend a helping hand, ear and heart.

Please do so with a COMPASSIONATE , LOVING, HEART selflessly because we sincerely wish to bring UNITY amongst us all, do it as a DUTY OF CARE

Everyone is on their own life journey, unknown moments occur where we don't always have the answers, there is no guide book, at times things may not go accordingly.

Some moments will make us, some will break us, we never stop learning.

There can be rough and tough times where we won't be able to turn back the hands of time or say "if only I could get another chance".

"GUESS WHAT.. Yes we have another chance and the moment is NOW.

Live life to the full like it's our last moment. Scream or yell, "I'M GOING TO LIVE EACH MOMENT TO THE FULL". Do what makes you HAPPY!

Never put off tomorrow for something that can be done today, we all have a right to be HAPPY, but not at the EXPENSE of another's HAPPINESS.

I am a fully qualified clinical hypnotherapist and a councillor with over 20 years of experience. My success rate is very high reaching out to people' in different countries.

My work is word of mouth, so when one benefits they tell another then another. I take my spiritual work very serious as I love and care about everything and all that there is. Should someone choose to reach out to me then it's VERY IMPORTANT to me that my connections succeeds for them to help them to be able to GAIN from contacting me.

If I am able to help another in any form or way then that is my success to see someone smiling laughing living their life to the full in health wealth peace joy happiness and most importantly UNITY. If my work works for me then why can it not work for you Beautiful souls out there. The affirmations are written in hypnotic manner that as you read them they can change your subconscious mind to get MORE FROM LIFE. No one needs to suffer in silence because we all have a FREE Will to reach out for HELP or GUIDANCE.

Each time you pick up this book you will find some new directions every time. It's like a little guide book to help us reach towards a more meaningful happy life. ENJOY the BOOK.

Love is the most precious pure gift we can ever give one another, it cannot be bought or sold or has a price tag. Love is so priceless beyond understanding, it is so divine which cannot be put into words, it can only be expressed or felt yet not touched.

Not many souls realise the value of love or the appreciation it deserves, it is so PURE that it cannot be taken for granted or be ABUSED.

We cannot give another what is not ours to give, so if we have not learnt to love our self then how can we give something we have not experienced. Learn to love our self first, love is the language of the HEART , could the heart be the SOUL.

There are so many things in life that cannot be bought, no matter how much wealth one can accumulate. Time health peace joy happiness . Especially relationships. Yes we need money, but not enough where we lose our focus on real reality. Of why we are here, on this Mother Earth, and for how long is something we have no idea. No guarantees. That is why it is so very important, to cherish every moment, everyone and everything . Do not let stress override us. Every moment is a Blessing. Make the very most of each moment. Smile, occasionally lose our selves in laughter. When was the last time we laughed so much, that our laughter uplifted the environment, and the souls in our company. Laughter is the best medicine that money can't buy.

Our time on this earth is so very short, that we don't realise this very valid reality. Don't take anyone or anything for granted. Cherish every moment as a priceless GIFT. That no money in the world can buy. Every morning is another birth and we should be so GRATEFUL. If we could learn to weigh up the value of our life, we would not wish to waste even a moment. Stop complaining. Instead count our BLESSINGS. Start LIVING and LOVING LIFE to the FULL. We may not be here tomorrow so don't waste today. We are all living on BORROWED TIME. What's borrowed does not belong to us, but we can make good use of it, to the full, by appreciating this time. We have to CARE and SHARE. Learn to LOVE, RESPECT EVERYONE and everything. KEEP SMILING and be HAPPY.

Why do most souls feel definition of love is receiving, others running around trying to fulfil all their needs and desires. Have we tried to understand or taken any steps to recognise what love actually is, and how love operates. Who is love better still what is love. Love is an inner deep feeling that can only be felt. It cannot be touched or seen. You can search but love cannot be found, it can be given by the ones who managed to manifest the compassionate, emotions of selfless feelings, created by our pure inner feelings and thoughts. Once we realise the value of pure divine love, all you want to do is give it out, share it out. Our hearts are so big that we can love the whole world should we choose to. Love is limitless it desires no return, it's so selfless and unconditional.

As soon as we judge and resent another, the thought immediately separates us. But when we send a loving, compassionate thought, it brings us together as one.

Love and resentment cannot flow side by side.

Compassion lifts our vibrations, while negative and insecure thoughts lower them. This impacts our mental state and overall health, causing emotional and mental stress.

It also creates blocks in our ability to manifest and receive positive things in our everyday lives.

That's why it is so important to maintain a good, healthy, positive, and compassionate state of mind.

When we uplift our thoughts and emotions by sending love and light to everyone in our lives, it brings us peace.

It's heartbreaking to see what is happening all around us. Every moment we are allowing distance to separate us from one another. Yet we are all meant to be united together as one. We need to ask our self. What is it that we want from life, remember we are here on BORROWED TIME. Think very carefully, and I pray we all choose what is highest for our highest good. Where we can bring peace joy harmony and UNITY. Please let's not SEPARATE our selves from one another. One day we are going to leave everyone we are judging and avoiding, or they may even go before our very eyes. Life is too short to spend in hatred blame and resentment, these emotions are POISON. Turn them into LOVE, and watch how LIFE BLOSSOM.

This may not resonate with all.

What type of energy are we forming, where there are so many compassionate kind understanding non judgemental souls, always on standby to reach out to anyone in need. Most of the population today is blinded by visions that may be suffering, but cannot see these souls, who wish to lend a helping hand and a listening ear.

Take pride and ego out, if it means one can benefit in some way or another. No one needs to suffer in silence, we need to seek and take the compassion that is available. No one needs to sit alone, and weep their TEARS in SILENCE, or in DARKNESS. Those tears and darkness, can IGNITE into LIGHT and LIFE, worth LIVING to the FULL. All it takes is to reach out and SEEK....

What is man ALONE, (nothing). Yet together we are EVERYTHING, we are nothing, yet everything. EGO is man's worst ENEMY. It overclouds one's natural normal personality. It can turn the most humble loving down to earth soul into unbearable being, where we begin to perhaps resent our own self. Kind consideration thoughts begin to fade away and vanish. Slowly bit by bit, we start losing our self to a point that if we were to look in the mirror, we will not recognise our own self. Being kind considerate and understanding plus non judgemental, shines a bright GLOW of DIVINE light through us, that radiates love and light where ever we go. Our COMPASSION, uplifts everyone's presence and touches so many HEARTS and LIVES.

Once we find that compassion to help others selflessly and unconditionally. So many good changes begin to occur within our consciousness self. We begin to loose our self to find a NEW PROFOUND person that was hidden within our self, due to the programming of the self centred method we have been programmed to live by. How many souls yearn to reach out to one another at times of need, without the other person asking for a helping hand. Helping others can bring us GREAT JOY and HAPPINESS, that can never be put into words or expressed. It's an uplifted vibration deep within that fill our eyes, with TEARS of JOY to sense and feel another's happiness. Share their pain and assure them that they are not alone.

The moment we learn to appreciate and love others, we no longer resonate with lower vibration thoughts (Negative). We begin to see GOOD in everyone around us, as there is good in everyone. At that point when our own VIBRATIONS begin to raise, we must learn to protect our frequency. We start feeling either tired or uplifted in others company. That is when we decide how much time we choose to share our company with others. When we are uplifted, we feel completely different, (positive happy). We start laughing more, our awareness sharpens so that we notice our surroundings. ENERGY is souls most valuable asset that operates us. Be WISE who we choose to share our energy with.

Every living soul is either a NEEDLE or a SCISSORS. A needle soul will spend all their time and effort being loving and compassionate, going out of its way being honest true and sincere. Finding every opportunity fulfilling others happiness, and patching RELATIONSHIPS TOGETHER. While the SCISSORS soul is very INSECURE, always on the look out for its own BENEFIT, putting Their own wants and needs first. They don't see or want 50/50. It's got to be more for them. They never stop searching as they have no limits. They will always come first, and to secure their own wants needs and desires. Their only form of guaranteed security is to CUT UP OTHER RELATIONSHIPS. Yet even after cutting other relationships, they still find NO PEACE or CONTENTMENT . So be very careful as karma will come around.

Once we have found Bliss, don't let it out of sight. Make it permanent. Along with it comes PEACE JOY HARMONY. We begin to stay in Constance peace of mind, nothing overrides us any more. When issues occur, as they regularly do, our peaceful mind is free that it finds solutions immediately. Without allowing any STRESS. Life becomes so BEAUTIFUL that we start to live life to the FULL, seeing BEAUTY everywhere. Suddenly life begins to AWAKEN us, from this deep sleep we are in at the moment, living to see each day with only one eye open, whilst the other eye is in DEEP sleep. Our real eye is our THIRD EYE (PINEAL GLAND). We are all Blessed to be able to open our third eye. Should we wish to do so. Remember we all have a free will.

Why do some souls hurt and belittle the ones who love them the most. This is the time line we are living on, where we can no longer identify right from wrong, fake from truth. The ones that love us wish to see us uplifted and happy, always on standby to help and encourage us to follow our dreams. Being our strength, sharing our stress and pain. They will never bring a TEAR of pain but a tear of Joy and laughter. They uplift us so high that the sky is the limit. Wanting nothing in return for making our happiness their own. Their love is unconditional and selfless. Even when we may end up hurting them, they stand ready just in case we fall, holding us up as a pillar of strength love and light, shining so radiant wiping all our flaws of darkness.

Souls who choose to vibrate on lower thoughts of vibrations, do not realise that by raising their vibrations, they can create such an amazing positive solid platform. Not only for them selves, but for their loved ones and the rest of the world. Even a very small positive gesture of compassion is a BIG CONTRIBUTION, to the whole cosmic universe. Everything is ENERGY and VIBRATIONS. Thoughts are very POWERFUL. Be very careful of what we allow into our subconscious mind, remember we are the master of our own mind. Learn to think for our selves by cutting out the inputs of others views and opinions. Unless they benefit us and others, in a good loving positive compassionate united feeling, of happiness and joy. They uplift us and not lower our vibrations, because we are judging a situation or a soul, by another's input that has overruled our own view.

What is LOVE, love is not linked with the mind body or senses, where there are strings conditions and expectations attached. Worldly love is attached to feelings and emotions, with a high and low sense of feelings. When we get our own way it shoots up high and when the opposite it drops low. Spiritual love is pure and divine, comes from the soul (ATMA). It has no conditions. It has a cosmic flow where you just want to radiate love and light, where ever you look and go. No strings no expectations but that feeling of wanting to radiate that magical substance, that cannot be seen. It brings out the best of our highest self beyond any means. Try loving others selflessly and unconditionally with no strings or expectations. Especially without a return.

How many have experienced both tears of joy and tears of heartache and pain?

The tears of pain cut like a knife—the pain is so unbearable, it's impossible to explain the symptoms you feel inside. Your whole world feels like it has collapsed and fallen apart.

However, the tears of gratitude and joy are entirely different. You close your eyes, and suddenly the noise and sound of the outside world fade away. All you feel is relaxed, blissful—your heartbeat slows down as you take slow, deep, comfortable breaths.

An angelic voice inside softly whispers:
"Hey… this is paradise. This is heaven."

And in that moment, you just want to stay in that transformational state of consciousness.

Believe me, you don't want to open your eyes - because you know you're about to step back into a world full of dramatic actions.

First learn to love ourselves, then learn to respect our selves. Respect has to be gained by others who are sincere souls. In the way we ACT and BEHAVE our ACTIONS and ATTITUDE towards other souls.
Only then are we able to identify our LOYALTY towards ourselves and others. Always put POLITENESS COMPASSION KINDNESS WISDOM TRUST TRUTH SINCERENESS and UNDERSTANDING, in front of our WALK and TALK. Think very carefully, on how we APPROACH each situation and circumstances . We should radiate an example by our ACTIONS. Never HURT or BELITTLE anyone. Let that KINDNESS and SOFTNESS flow out from our SOUL to ERASE another's HEARTACHE PAIN OR SADNESS.

As foolish or as silly as it may sound, I love and care about everything THAT THERE IS. If I have been blessed to walk on this Mother Earth, she has very carefully and smartly provided everything and anything that was needed. Just before I entered my mother's womb, I felt shy and said "where's my clothes and my belongings". The cosmic divine voice said. Everything is ready and waiting there for you, even your clothes. However, when you return back, you will come back exactly as you are leaving Empty handed. You will bring no belongings back with you, and you will be able to gather and accumulate as much as you wish but nothing will return back with you on your return. Whilst you are there make sure you spread a lot of love and light along with unity. There are lots of souls there may not like you or wish to befriend you. At times you may feel very lonely and sad as not many souls will understand who you are. On earth they only befriend the body and not the soul. You may end up crying so many weeping tears trying to adapt and to fit in with their similar vibrations. You must love respect and care for all that there is. BE KIND, CONSIDERATE, UNDERSTANDING AND NON-JUDGEMENTAL. Don't befriend NEGATIVITY, EGO, ANGER, RESENTMENT, HATE, SEPARATION and the list went on. The next minute I am in a very dark place full of liquid where I am fed with a tube going into my belly. I had no one to talk to or play with. Occasionally I could hear sounds coming from the other side, good job I was given patience to be NOTHING yet EVERYTHING. One day I saw this illuminate light so bright that it got me screaming and crying, because the light I was used to was so calming and soothing like the sound of harps playing constantly. Should one choose to listen. From that day on

I was wrapped in a cloth and fed milk, which I found hard to resonate with. I got bigger and discovered something different and new every moment. Some nice some not so nice things events and incidents, but my strength and courage helped me to cope in the best way I knew how. When I left the realm I came from. I came naked and empty handed with nothing, but I forgot to hang the LOVE on the hanger as I was not supposed to bring anything with me. That love in my heart started to grow. I had to make it a home in my heart as there was nowhere else I could hide it. The bigger my love was growing I knew I had to spread it by giving bit by bit away. So, I tried to share it with others but not many wanted to take a piece or a portion of my love from me. I would speak to Mother Earth crying almost every night, trying so hard to understand why I was sent to a place where not many souls wanted to care or share especially the love I was carrying in my heart. I was so desperate to share it with everyone, but not many wanted a piece of my PURE DIVINE LOVE. My love was so SELFLESS and UNCONDITIONAL. All I wanted to do was give and give as I had great pleasure from giving, from young age.

I had pleasure of going around to the elderly ladies who lived alone in our street and would buy their required items from the corner shop. I remember one lady regular list was snuff for her nose to sniff and a bottle of cider, that day I was running and somehow slipped and fell breaking her bottle of cider. I picked up the biggest piece of the glass. I handed her the snuff and showed her the piece of glass of what had happened, she burst out crying as she had no cider. I thought for a moment trying to connect with her sad emotions at that time. Luckily, I had some pennies spare as, at that time the value of money was higher than it is today, so I was able to run home, pick up the pennies and buy her another bottle of cider. My heart was full of love that was desperate to flow out from my heart that I had to find ways to share it with those who were in need of my type of spiritual love.

I did not want anything in exchange for sharing it. I had to get rid of it as it was getting bigger and bigger expanding day by day. I loved everyone everything and all that there is. Not many loved me back in the way I knew how to love, which was selfless and unconditional love, and I could not understand why, not many wanted to befriend me or wanted to know me as the person of who I really was.

We are three people. The one we think we are. The one others think we are, and the one we really are. I tried my best to remind myself, every moment of the promise I made to be KIND, CONSIDERATE, UNDERSTANDING AND NON JUDGEMENTAL. So many souls took my love so wrong. My love was not linked with the mind the body or the senses. My love was spiritual love, that was PURE and DIVINE, expecting or wanting NOTHING in return. Most of my life I felt very alone as no one has understood or got to know me for whom I am. Instead, everyone has only seen and judged me from their own frequency and vibrational energies. I grew up in a large family, who loved but a separated love where you come first then the others are second. This type of love is not united love by putting one's own self first. This becomes ARROGANT and EGOISTIC love. It became even more distant as my brothers got married and their wives entered into my worldly family's circle; different divisions began to occur as they did not know or perhaps want unity amongst each other. My birth mother was a weak soul, governed and over powered by my birth father, so together the EGOS expanded over ruling our household. Because of this type of energies and vibrations, throughout my life I felt excluded and misunderstood, which many times was heart breaking and I cried so many tears as to why was I excluded. Although I was wise, maybe not wise enough to know that my energies and vibrations were not similar to all the others around me, and they still are not the same even today. Now I have begun to understand as to why I was not invited to my own family functions. Not one soul in my family ever spoke up for me each time I was pushed aside or not invited to a gathering where the rest were invited. It was never addressed what was right and what was wrong. Many times, I tried to speak and have a heart to heart with my mother as to why was I being excluded from being invited to family gatherings. The fact was not that I was not invited but the reasons, my mind and heart was asking to hear from the others point of view or opinions, so that I could begin to have an understanding of their reasons for excluding me. Also that I could have a closure of knowing for my own feelings and emotions to know and accept. I would say to my mother I have a right to know the Reasons as to why they are doing this to me so that I can at least try to UNDERSTAND. Even up till this moment not one family member has approached me to give me a good reason or an answer to this question. However, as time has gone by, I have learnt that there is no right or wrong, no good or bad. We are all different individuals with a different thinking concept and life of different choices. So, if anyone does not wish to be in my company, then I have learnt to accept their decision, through respect to them I realise that WE ALL HAVE A FREE WILL . Although I do spend time and love seeing my family the connection still is not on the same frequency, there are many things I wish to speak, ask share question on a different energy and vibrational frequency, but I am unable to do so. I have a much better understanding spiritual connection with the new younger frequency that my nieces' nephews and their children carry, as we are reaching the GOLDEN AGE.

Where UNITY will once again start returning amongst one another, especially with the INDIGOS RAINBOWS and CRYSTAL souls who walk amongst us. All on this cosmic universe who, together have been changing the vibrations and energies that has changed the frequencies of the whole cosmic universe, getting the stage ready for unity to play its role. We are all cosmic children who have come on this earth to play our roles in this big playground called EARTH. There is not enough unity and all my life

I have longed and yearned for UNITY. Luckily the cosmic universe has bought some special souls (although every soul is special). Into my life that are my life and I love them so very much, and feel blessed to have them in my life as a GIFT. That I cherish every moment sending them lots of love and light. Therefore, I will never take them for granted. Where I come from, we do everything from LOVE, with love for love. I do not know anything else except HOW TO LOVE OTHERS and ALL THAT THERE IS. Maybe this is to do with the love I accidentally bought into this cosmic world with me and it lives inside of me each and every moment. Perhaps if I had remembered to hang my love and left it behind before I came here, then perhaps others may have excepted me into their lives and not judged or excluded me like I have been. All my life almost everyone took from me with one hand and then pushed me away from themselves with their other hand. Not one person has taken a moment or the time to understood me of who and what I am. I am nothing yet everything. I have nothing to give accept my love which is pure and divine, it's ETERNAL AWAKENED LOVE that never DIES. My love will never die because we are all love and light. Maybe just maybe the cosmic universe wished for me to bring this love with me, maybe they sent it with me because they knew I was not going to be accepted by many souls and that I was going to be excluded from the rest.

I sit here and laugh and say to myself out aloud that not many souls wanted my love or wished to share it with me and that is comical and still puts a smile on my face and makes me laugh. All I know is that, I do not own anything other than this love I carry in my heart that no one seems to want to share with me. Love is COMPASSION, it comes from the soul and can only be accepted by another soul. This spiritual love is very PURE DIVINE and is ETERNAL. There will come a time here on earth very soon where almost every soul will think act and behave with the soul and not the MIND BODY or the SENSES, and the time is not very far away. This world is very big, yet it feels very lonely and small. Everyone is out for themselves. Filling their bank balances, everything here is about status name and fame. Material things, I see beautiful souls running around accumulating money and wealth without taking a moment to realise that there is nothing here that belongs to us, or that we will be able to take anything with us, when we leave this earth plane. Everything that exists here is given to us to use to the full. We will be gone one day, yet everything else shall remain here even, after we have gone. THERE IS NOTHING HERE ON THIS EARTH PLANE THAT DOES NOT HAVE A SELL BY DATE (including us). So why not start to live our life to the full by start living, and stop accumulating unnecessary things we may not even need but have enough to keep us going. More importantly start living. Remember why we are here. To be free spirits happy smiling playing around without a care in the world, stress free. To help and uplift one another, to be another's vision and strength, to care and share. Yes we have to go to work but accumulate enough where time is spent wisely with loved ones. Live for ourselves too as we do not know when our calling will arrive and everything and everyone else will be left behind here. Nothing is more HEARTBREAKING than to have not lived your life to the full. Learn to take it easy. Find things to smile and laugh about. Use our compassion and wisdom more wisely, more often. We are all ONENESS. No one is separate from anything or anyone. I plead with all my heart PLEASE let's bring UNITY back into our awesome beautiful magical lives and play like the innocent children we all are. So FULL of GRACE and COMPASSION. Let's not let another soul go through life all alone excluded by groups formed by judgemental accusations that were and are not true. Because of our EGOS and ARROGANCE. Yes I hold my hands up that I have made some silly errors trying to fit in so desperately wanting to be accepted. That's when I have dropped my energy vibrations low to fit in. Guess what, was I able to fit in. No, instead I allowed others to use me, taking full advantage of my good nature. Taking from me with one hand and then pushing me away with the other hand. I could see everything that was happening but my heart overruled my head with the same thought, popping up each time. THAT YOU COULD BE GONE TOMORROW and EVERYTHING WILL BE LEFT BEHIND, so I would walk away as I have never liked CONFRONTATIONS. It was easier for me to walk away from situations and circumstances, to keep my peace of mind. From young age I have not ALLOWED MONEY or MATERIAL THINGS TO OVERRULE my HEAD. All I know is that the cosmic universe has always said to me, "You have to be honest true and sincere. When we send you into another's life. The test is not for you but for them ". So I try my best to be honest true and sincere. I will never hurt anyone intentionally. I have never befriended anyone because I wanted anything from them. I love and respect everyone. Even the ones who has judged and left me. I still care and love them all, and whenever they need me, I will be there for them at times of need. Without them asking me but as my duty of care towards humanity, to offer my help without being asked for, by them.

However, at the same time I will no longer allow anyone to use me, as there is helping and being used and that is not helping. I have learnt that we can love others from afar. My love is DETACHED LOVE. With no strings conditions or expectations. It's selfless without a return of exchange. Ever since I was young, I knew I had a purpose for coming on this earth but I never knew what. From 21st December 2012 the universe started giving me little by little to how much I could handle the reasons as to why they sent me here. Then in 2018 whilst in meditation (as I do meditate a lot and also teach meditation). I was taken to 3 different realms as an observer. One was very uncomfortable to watch and see but I am willing to share the experience of all that I saw and watched, only by speaking in person to anyone who is ready to hear as it is not for everyone, as we are all on different levels of vibrations and timelines. The second realm was very similar to the first but not as bad, as the first one was. I was able to see more there and spent I can't say time, as time is man made and does not exist there, but I know how much I saw what I could bare to see. The last realm really hit me the most and changed me completely as a person that I am today, (remember I am a spiritual being, having a human experience). We went through these massive big tall golden gates, I couldn't see the sun but it was very beautiful and bright, calming and peaceful. The grass was so soft under my feet like a cushion as I was not wearing any shoes and the reason, I know this is because I was feeling the softness of the green grass under my feet. To the left and right was little shinning bulbs (like Christmas lights). They were all different colours but I could hear them laughing in bliss communicating with one another through laughter. I saw two paths, one to the left but we took the one to the right. My guardian Angel who was mostly as a white shining light but every now and again I could see a faint aura of wings and the shape and form of an angel as bright shining light. The other two walked in a floating slow sliding movement that was so magical and soothing to watch. They did not speak. The angel said the path on the left takes you to a place, where souls who had addictions on earth or were severely ill, have to take a long rest to recoup, until they are allowed to go where we were heading for. I saw these tall figures of shinning white light so tall. Very faintly I could see something on their heads like the ends of a rolling pin. I couldn't see whether it was something on their heads to cover it or a halo. They each had scrolls with them. Each scroll was from every different life time we have lived or existed. One scroll, when rolled out could be seen spread out as miles and miles long. Written on there by our own consciousness of our every thought action and deeds of karma, that is taken into account. I saw that even having a good or negative thought is still counted for, and not just actions as karma. There was a soul being judged. The voice asked: you were on earth for 85 years what did you do. The soul did not know what to say so the same question was asked 3 times, each time in more authoritative raised consciousness voice. We were all connected together as energy form of communication by our consciousness. Like cotton wool, at times it was like tracing paper then it would change again to white very thin layers of white energy.

(I can still see the very same energy here since my return back on earth). The first answer was given, I had 3 children and I bought them this and that, immediately the consciousness cut in. You were on earth for 85 years what did you do. My heart sank because I was feeling and connected to the emotions of the conversation taking place. The soul looked to the left then to the right and thought, the ones I lied for and allowed myself to do, and be drawn into situations of making karma for myself are not even here with me. Most of my karma was accumulated for my loved ones and here I am standing all alone taking it all upon myself. What the consciousness was asking was, what did you do for a third person SELFLESS DEEDS is what really counts as we are all connected together as ONENESS. What we do for our families is a DUTY that should be done to the full. What they take into account is what we do for others selflessly and unconditionally who are not worldly related to us. The soul bowed its head down and fell down on its knees, when it realised what the question was, and that the ones who were a part of their karma was not even there with them. The 85 years on EARTH were wasted and that he or she (remember our soul has no age or gender) did not do what was expected from them to carry out, to do as to what and why they were sent down on earth to do. Was to be KIND, COMPASSIONATE, CONSIDERATE, UNDERSTANDING, UNITED, WISE, TRUTHFUL and non-judgemental. I heard the sobs of weeping and crying getting loader. Please give me another chance to go back and do what I was meant to do. At that very moment it hit me, that I was not prepared to leave Earth to come here and to beg to be given another chance to put right what should have been done in the first place. So, I promised myself that I am going to do what is expected from me selflessly and unconditionally right now immediately, and not wait for another life time. At that very moment. I woke up from my meditation. Ever since that moment of time, I do not know as to whether the universe sent another different soul in my body, but I am a completely different changed person (soul). I do not remember everything about my past, but when I do meet people here on earth, the universe gives me little clues of past events with them that I can communicate with them on their level, but lots of things people close to me talk about we have done together and places visited ext. I have no collection of, as I cannot remember so I just listen and say nothing. However, many times I ask myself. WHO AM I, WHAT AM I. The voice inside says SUPREME DIVINE LOVE AND LIGHT. You have come here TO TOUCH PEOPLES HEARTS and LIVES, mostly to bring UNITY. To set by EXAMPLE, Spread LOVE and LIGHT. All I know is that I love everyone everything and all that there is. I do not live in the past but in the present moment. I do not blame anyone for anything and have no resentment towards anyone. When others do me wrong, I forgive them immediately and send them lots of love and light, however I don't forget so that they cannot do it to me again. I am not on this earth to win brownie points but to be honest, true and sincere is very important to me. So, if someone was to ask me my purpose on this earth plane, I am happy to answer immediately. To radiate and share love, peace, joy, harmony, happiness and unity, to care and share, uplift one other. Become another's strength. More than anything else. To bring UNITY BACK HERE. Only unity compassion and love can save this BEAUTIFUL WORLD and it's AMAZING PEOPLE (souls). Especially when you LOVE them so much and so deeply with all your HEART. (The whole world is my family). I am ONLY LOVE and LIGHT, I could never ever HURT another, even if I wanted to. My father is watching my every move, action deed and word. I will always focus only on the reasons I have come down to do, is to bring souls together, to wipe another's TEARS, to uplift them, encourage them to never give up. We all have a right to be happy as long as we are not hurting harming or stealing. Doing anything that's low vibrational, that is not good for our highest good. Only do what is good for our highest good and the good of others. Allow our conscience to lead and guide us, should we lose our path of righteousness. Never ever hurt, use or abuse another, no matter what. Although I love everyone. I do not love others for gains to receive. The universe provides me with everything I need even more than I need. I am so grateful that I cannot thank them enough. This is for looking after me, keeping me safe, watching over me, protecting me and for providing my every need. I am very happy and content, seeing everyone else are also happy and healthy in their own homes, what more could I ask for. I came on my own with nothing (although I bought love in my heart). I will leave with nothing. I have not come on this earth plane to take anything away from anyone but came to give. Neither have I come to hurt anyone, I am not perfect (perfect is just a word in the dictionary and does not exist in reality). I do not know everything either, we never stop learning. This is why EARTH IS A SCHOOL FOR LEARNING AND TEACHING LESSONS. Remember one importance's of the reasons as to why we have come here on EARTH at this time, is to bring PEACE JOY HARMONY AND UNITY.

Once you have read this book you may start to look at life circumstances and situations from your HEART and not your MIND. The mind can play GAMES but the heart never LIES. Life is a GAME play it. Life is a CHALLENGE, meet it. Life is a DREAM realise it. This will guide you to LOVE life to the FULL from your HEART.